Conversations with a Ol' Wise Dude

As told by The Ol' Wise Dude

Anonymous

For permission requests, email the publisher, with the subject line "Attention: Permissions Coordinator," at the email address below.
www.duschamgt.com

ISBN 978-0-9983738-1-2

First Edition 2016

Conversations with a Ol' Wise Dude
As told by The Ol' Wise Dude

Written by Anonymous

Published by Duscha Management LLC
www.duschamgt.com

CONTENTS

ACKNOWLEDGMENTS

Acknowledgment to all the wise people that have spoken wisdom and breathed life into teaching, mentoring, coaching, and instructing those who needed their intervention and intelligence.

DEDICATION

This book is dedicated to all the elders, storytellers, sages, and wise ones that have shared their infinite wisdom with us all.

1

CHAPTER – MISCELLANEOUS WISDOM

"I know you know the story of the scorpion and the frog? The scorpion asks the frog to carry him across a river. The frog is afraid of being stung, but the scorpion reassures him that if it stung the frog, they both would drown. The frog agrees; nevertheless, in mid-river, the scorpion stings him, dooming the two of them. When asked why, the scorpion explains, "I'm a scorpion; it's my nature."

"If you learn the difference between temporary loses and defeat, you will learn that the seeds of success begin with a grateful heart."

"Some people will be your friend because of who you know. Some people will be your friend because of your position. Some people will be your friend because of the way you look. Some people will be your friend because of your possessions. But real friends are those who will be your friends because they like who you are on the inside."

"There is no substitute for paying attention to your surroundings. So when the bad things in life happen, it reflects you failing to open your eyes to the good things that you weren't paying attention to before."

"I don't know what love is for everyone, but I can tell you what it is for me; love is knowing all about someone, and still wanting to be with them more than any other person, love is trusting them enough to tell them everything about yourself, including what you're ashamed of, love is feeling comfortable and safe with someone, but still getting weak when they walk into a room and smile at you."

Do not deny the love that is given to you because you fear loss or pain, or your life will be empty and your loss greater"—
African Proverb

"The most beautiful thing about life is that we have choices. We get to choose our reaction for each and every situation that happens. We can choose to be positive and believe that good things are going to happen. Or we can choose to be negative... No matter what we choose to believe, it affects us and how we live life."

"People tend to be so worried about what they eat between Christmas and the New Year, but really people, really, you ought to be worried about what you eat between New Year's Day and Christmas."

"People must trust themselves. Mom always said if you don't believe in YOU, how in the hell you expect someone else to? Real Talk: If you don't believe in you, you'll spend your entire life looking for someone else to prove your merit and validate you. WOW. And the end result is YOU will never be satisfied. WOW. So in the end you will be asking for validation and resenting the feedback at the same time."

"A dude much wiser than myself once told me "A successful marriage requires falling in love many times, but always with the same person.""

"Always embrace the good things in your life...The air you breathe, the people who surround you, the culture you evolve from...the spirit that fills your soul, and makes you who you truly are. They could be your own! Lift your head high - and shout, sing, praise, and live this life to the fullest...you only have one!"

"Joyfulness keeps your heart and your face looking youthful. Each day we should strive to secure a good laugh. It will make you a better friend, make you happier with yourself, and positively impact everyone around you."

"I really think we need to cleanse some folks that just haven't prepared their fruit. They talk a good game, when their fruit is spoiled before it even dropped from the tree. If a child is out here causing DRAMA in the community then you better check that tree."

"If you believe you must struggle for abundance, then your situations in life will be conducive to struggle If you believe you cannot experience love without pain, then the universe will give you exactly that - love with pain."

"Sometimes when people are in need and you tell them something that they NEED to hear, they do not listen, they do not respond, because they would rather get some advice from a FOOL."

"Everyone who has ever done a kind deed for us, or spoken a word of encouragement to us, has entered into the make-up of our character and our thoughts, as well as our success."

"The difference between good people and bad people is good people do the right thing when no one else is looking."

"We all need to smile at each other, smile at our wives and husbands, smile at our children, hell just smile at each other. At the end of the day we will all benefit from a greater love for each other."

"Instead of complaining about stuff think about this. When we long for life without difficulties, we should be reminded that oak trees grow strong in contrary winds and diamonds are created under pressure."

"Love is when the other person's happiness is more important than your own."

"Lack of self-love is the most common source of emotional pain and baggage. If someone feels insecure, unworthy and lack of value, their core may not allow them to experience real love when they find it."

"A wise man once said "Survival is not our most basic instinct, it is family. If you asked most people they'd give up their life to save a member of their family. But most of us live our lives taking family for granted"

"Sometimes you gotta allow someone to be free in order to be free yourself."

"Children naturally mimic what they see their parents do, so no matter what you say, they do what they see. So based on some adults behavior, bad parenting been around much longer than you think."

"A common mistake many folks have made when trying to make something totally foolproof is they underestimate the ingenuity of complete fools."

"I remain thankful for the gifts that I've been given and I try to use them in a good way, in a positive way."

"The apple doesn't fall far from the tree. Therefore the apple tells the truth about the tree. If you want the truth about the apple just examine the tree it fell from."

"When two people meet, there's really more people present. There is how each person sees themselves, each person as they desire to be seen, and each person as who they truly are."

"When presented with potential conflict and strife, you must keep your compass near for it will always lead you in the right direction."

"If everything that happens is never our fault, we don't have to take responsibility for it. If you can't take responsibility for it, you'll always consider yourself a victim."

"The people we are in relationship with are always a mirror, reflecting our own beliefs, and simultaneously we are mirrors, reflecting their beliefs.

"Do this. Take some time and reflect and rejuvenate. Some amazing things are revealed to you when you give yourself space and time."

"A wise man once said that bluffing is not lying. For instance, you might act like a wealthy person because you realize that the acting will eventually make you wealthy."

"Why do some people stay shady even when they way too old to be? Just when you give someone a chance to "come correct" the shady just pours out."

"Life has seasons, so don't get all caught up in what other people are doing. There's this thing about seasons, they always change."

"What most people need to learn in life is how to love people and use things instead of using people and loving things."

"Fill yourself up with fun, humor, and good will and you'll become a magnet for more of the same."

"At the end of the day, real friends will help you, and casual acquaintances reveal themselves."

"A relationship is one of the most powerful tools for personal growth."

"Handle your business, cause worrying about other people's business will get your business handled by someone else."

"I'm at a point in life where everything I do is primarily for the service of others. I will worry about me later."

"If you really want to find out what kind of person you are-try helping someone improve their quality of life."

"One of the things that really shows the character of a man is what he laughs at."

"Don't mistake kindness for weakness. Kindness isn't weak. Kindness is a certain type of strength."

"Former mayor of Detroit Coleman Young once said, "You can't look forward and backward at the same time."

"Be careful who you allow in your circle. Some people you got to love from afar."

"They say that He who wants to barter, usually knows what is best for him."

"Grandma always said son, do more GOOD than HARM and you will always be blessed."

"In reality, wise men learn more from fools than fools do from a wise man."

"Never ever waste time playing the woulda shoulda coulda game."

"It's not how you enter the room, but how energize and impact it before you leave"

"You cannot misquote silence."

"We waste a lot of time chasing folks that we could have caught by just standing still."

"You're lucky if you have three friends for life."

"Do me a favor and don't do me no favors."

"Sometimes it is what it is. The truth can be harsher than a lie."

"Sometimes it's not WHAT you do but WHEN you do it."

"If only leafy green vegetables smelled as good as bacon."

"Everything ain't for everybody."

2

CHAPTER – COACHING, WELLNESS AND PERSONAL DEVELOPMENT

"Everyone has a skill set. Every skill set can be re-tooled into a positive personal strategy for success. Sometimes people have a natural talent but fight against it because of what they want to do versus what they should do. Their goals are not aligning with their values. Sometimes people are afraid to ask for help with developing their natural talent. My advice is to be coachable, be willing to critically assess what needs to be changed in you to elevate your existence"

"Do you want to know the difference between coaching and mentoring? Nothing!"

"Leadership is lifting someone's vision of themselves to a higher place. It is raising their thinking and self-worth to its rightful place. No more settling for lame or sorry or under achieving folks. If you really value self then expect to get the best, expect a King/Queen and be ready to handle the responsibility that goes along with it. You won't keep something that you don't earn."

"To get a new outcome you must do things in a new way. So visualize yourself achieving your goals if you want to make them happen."

"You can motivate players better with kind words than you can with a whip. My philosophy when I coached was if people gotta whip your ass then you not really ballin'. Some coaches only know how to yell and they lose good players for not recognizing who you can do what to. When I played you only had to whip me once and one time only."

"All players are created equal, some just work harder than others. I challenge you today to ask yourself what are you willing to sacrifice in order to improve your game?"

"A team will reflect the attitude of the Coach. For a positive, upbeat team, you gotta portray that image to the team. Good Coaches present positives, keep everybody focused and focused on the goals. And they show the example for everyone else to follow. If someone doesn't follow the example, then they don't deserve to be there. Period."

"Whenever you're in conflict with someone, there is one factor that can make the difference between damaging your relationship and deepening it. That factor is attitude."

"Some people are never going to win at anything because they expect the victory without following the RULES required that prepare you for the win. And there are rules. People running around claiming Victory when they can't follow simple rules. Winning has never occurred by accident."

"Regular and vigorous exercise is the medicine for creating change in a person's physical, emotional, and mental states. If you think that you do not have time for regular exercise sooner or later you will have to find time for illness."

"Good leaders must first become good servants." As a leader, remember your role in making sure the team gets served. Your reward is from a higher place as the service to others outweighs everything in the end. Remain grounded in what the other people get from you."

"Nothing gives me more joy than the amazing feeling of helping and watching friends pursue and achieve goals they have set for themselves. Sometimes all we need is someone who believes in our ability and talents and lets us know it."

"As a poker player, it ain't about having good cards, it's about playing the bad hands well. I have seen many a good card hand lose to a weaker hand. Tell you what, you may be Ace-King diamond suited, but let 3-5-7 clubs fall and I am sitting on a 4-6 in the big blind."

"When they are winning, no one says anything. As soon as they lose, everybody has something to say. There is an old saying that a winner listens, and losers wait for a turn to talk. There is no sure fire key to success, but the key to failure is trying to please everybody."

"Choose to take the calculated risk, to dream, to build, to fail or succeed. I choose to work harder than the next man. Choose to sweat till exhaustion. Choose the challenge against the top competition. Don't trade winning without the satisfaction of battle."

"There are times when you want to get better at your craft so you must get better alone. I call it Putting in work in the Closet. Everyone does not have to see or know what you are working on, but when you get back into the game as they say YOU GOT BETTER."

"If you truly aspire for success then be grateful for what you have, however little you may think it is, it is far greater than many others. And do not resent life as if it owes you something. Only you owe you something."

"When a player runs the play exactly the way a coach orders, it isn't ballin'. It's following instructions. Anyone with the physical qualifications can do that. Real players adjust to what the defense gives them."

"Choices means giving UP something you want, for something you want MORE."

"Funny thing about going far in life is, you have to be nice to young people, understanding with old people, sympathetic with poor folks, and tolerant of arrogant folks. In life we are all of these at some point."

"Every player I speak with all WANT the same thing. Well if I were to gauge your Want To would I see the work results in the prize? Do you give in to that voice telling you that you are too tired to work out today?"

"Keep your eyes focused on being better tomorrow than you are today."

"You have to take pride in your craft, don't let a blessing that you've been given die off. Teach others so that they may identify their blessing. So many of the kids just need someone to help them see the light."

"Look at a loss as an opportunity disguised. Let's face it, a single loss is a temporary defeat. You must be smart enough to recognize your weaknesses but still remember to do what got you to the dance."

"Wherever you go, whatever you do, if you are rude, then you are wrong."

"We were created with a purpose. Most do not know how to make the investment to fulfill that purpose. There are no shortcuts as everything requires a sacrifice as a part of the preparation"

"Believe in yourself! Have faith in your abilities! We cannot expect others to believe in us if we do not believe in ourselves. But keep in mind that we must remain humble in our confidence."

"Good teamwork is like an orchestra. Therefore Soloist need NOT apply."

"I once heard the great coach Chuck 'Daddy Rich' Daly say The first shot does not beat you." I agree. Because if I were still coaching a team right now, I would stop practice every time a player did not box out."

"The coach has tremendous influence, either good or bad, on the education of student-athletes and, thus, should never place winning above the value of instilling character."

"Coaches come and go, players you work out with come and go, but parents are the one constant!"

"You have worked too hard to allow anyone to discount your ability. Play above the mediocrity and stay focused on developing your skills."

"Appreciate what we're lucky enough to have while we're lucky enough to have it. Trust me, there is always someone waiting for their luck to change."

"You play the way you practice. This is true for both sports and life. Practice full speed yet under control. The muscle memory you develop determines the outcome."

"No one can make you feel insignificant, unless you allow them to. Keep your power and don't give it up so easily. It is a gift that once you give up---it is hard to get back."

"Positive energy leads to more positive energy. Check the energy of those around you and you will see how this works."

"Remember that sacrifices are not punishment so there is no excuse that exists which can keep you from greatness. Nothing. No one. No situation."

"The real key to being healthy is not diet, or exercise, or habits. It is about your reaction to challenges and rejecting stressors."

"Set a goal of doing more good than harm, of being more positive than negative, of helping others more than you need help."

"Winners stay balanced because you must keep your focus no matter the position you find yourself in. In the end you will triumph."

"Beware of those with no priorities, with no agenda for their own lives, they have nothing to lose by destroying yours."

"As you walk down the fairway of life you must smell the flowering trees, for you only get to play one round."

"If your actions inspire others to dream more, learn more, do more and become more, you are a leader."

"Let your optimism attract others to you."

"Game recognizes game and you're looking awfully unfamiliar at this moment."

"Is your Want To strong enough to make you successful? Do you really want something or just say you do?"

"Everything is attainable if you believe in yourself first, as you cannot expect others to believe in something that you don't."

"It is hard to maintain focus, as the weak mind is always attracted to the shiny and glittery things."

"A shark never closes its eyes, even when attacking. Once the pressure is put on, there is no release of that pressure."

"Why you calling for the ball if you not ready to shoot."

"If you feel good about it do it, you got ONE SHOT to be you."

"In order to do what you want to do, you must be willing to do what you have to do."

"Don't make resolutions, make lifestyle changes."

"One thing about losers is they become bitter when behind and careless when ahead."

"Dumb loses more than Smart wins."

"Bad shooters are always open"

3

CHAPTER – MONEY AND INVESTMENTS

"Due to budget cuts new rules take effect Jan 1st, on the dress code: 1) Employees are advised to come to work dressed according to salary. 2) If we see you wearing Prada shoes and carrying a Gucci bag, we will assume you are doing well financially and therefore do not need a raise. 3) If you dress poorly, you need to learn to manage your money better, so that you can buy nicer clothes, so therefore you do not need a raise."

"You just can't fix stupid has been said by many a wise dudes throughout time."

"There are many people who think that Money will do everything. Well allow me to clarify. There are many of you who will do anything /and everything) for Money. Commit to doing things for the love of doing them and the Money becomes a by-product of the KARMA you just created for yourself and those who align in spirit with you."

"A wise man once said "the secret to success is seeing your work primarily as a service to others, and not as a means of personal gain.""

"When you get new opportunities, new associates, new exposure, there is a price to pay. That price is old opportunities, old associates, and the same old exposure. So embrace whatever takes YOU to a place that improves YOU, because no one gets there ALONE."

"Take the first step towards getting where you really want to be in life by deciding to not stay where you are, with the people you been staying around and get out and maximize your involvement with those who GIVE rather than TAKE."

"The people who soar in life are those that refuse to sit back and wait for things to happen and wish for change. Matter of fact, those who soar visualize in their minds that they are not going to quit in the face of a challenge, they commit to not letting anything hold them down."

"If your entire world is about status symbol type stuff, then the balance of the Universe has a natural order type of way of correcting that in other words you will never have anything of REAL substance because your energy is focused on the things that really do not matter"

"It is not about just being satisfied with what you have, it's deeper than that. Be careful of getting caught up in wanting things that you don't have and losing sight of the fact that what you already possess is a treasure most would give their eyeteeth to have."

"So many people have vices, I mean most people do something, but if your vice has such control over you that you choose to spend your last 5 dollars on it instead of say - getting something to eat or putting gas in your car, then you are in bad shape"

"If you want to be happy with money then you must first be happy without it. Once that happens the money comes when you not even focused on making it. The blessings just flow and flow and ALL that you touch seems to generate income."

"You just can't expect to get what you wish for, you only get what you work for. Many people don't realize what working for it really means. Working for it often means changing your thoughts about the definition of "working for it."

"Everybody wants to get paid!"

"If you truly aspire for success then be grateful for what you have, however little you may think it is, it is far greater than many others. And do not resent life as if it owes you something. Only you owe you something."

"The old saying it's not personal its business no longer applies. From now on its personal business. So please understand that executive decisions occur when I look out for my personal over your business.

"If you not generous with a meager income, how can you be generous with abundance"

"Today, and every day, deliver more than you are getting paid to do. The victory within success is halfway won if you learn the secret of putting out more than is expected of you. Be thankful for the opportunity."

"Everyone at some point in their life thinks they can change the world, but no one thinks of changing themselves. More important than money, material possessions or fame, how about TRUTH."

"Some people manage life like a monthly bill, while others are pay-as-you-go!"

"My grandmother once told me the lack of money is the root of all evil and not the other way around. Therefore if you are great at something never do it for free."

"Whatever you choose to focus your mind on becomes critical to your success because you will become what you think about most of the time."

"Do not fall subject to unconditional consumerism, the younger generations seem to be watching many of us believe in buying STUFF that in the end doesn't matter."

"Some things just don't go on sale...the real thing is never marked down...real stuff requires you to recognize what is authentic."

"My grandmother used to tell me to navigate righteously and quietly as you do not have to broadcast when you are doing great things. Just do them."

"Sometimes you have to acknowledge "that's too rich for my blood" and realize that simplistic has more resolve than flamboyant."

"You are only your own number one priority so stay on top of your business and stay on top of your life."

"The area of your life that you neglect to develop will always feed your insecurity. Face your fears and welcome growth."

"Every time money comes your way, you don't have to take it. Some money is the devil's money."

"A delayed blessing does not mean it is denied."

"No one is going to save you therefore you must create opportunities that result in self-reliance."

"When you green you grow, when you ripe you right."

"We must invest in self before others can invest in us.

"Upgrade your Values to Upgrade your Existence."

"It has been said that you cannot keep the gold that you didn't earn."

"If it's not right for your mind, body or spirit then you have to be willing to walk away."

"You cannot be blessed in the future if you need the past to bless you today."

4

CHAPTER –

Faith and Divine Intervention

"Be thankful for all of the gifts of LIFE. For every gift that has been presented to us, there is someone who has never been blessed. And blessings are a gift from GOD. There are times in which our resolve is tested in order to determine future blessings. Anger or harshness can destroy the spirit of those who have blessed us, and we ALL need to be blessed from time to time. When we are grateful for the good that has already occurred, we attract more good into our life. On the other hand, when we are ungrateful, we tend to shut ourselves off from the good that would have continued to come our way."

"What YOU are looking for is looking for YOU." Going a little bit deeper, when it finds you don't be afraid to accept it. Blessings from PAIN only come around ONCE and if YOU don't embrace it and love it and hold onto it, it will never come back. Don't be afraid to get what you think you should have, or YOU will never get it."

"Ain't nothing wrong with being a dreamer, sometimes you have to be the first one to see it. Long before you get what you want in the world, it manifests from your heart and mind. So dream and believe it-and it will happen."

"What you are seeking is seeking you. If what you are seeking is in alignment with who you are and what you truly desire (versus what you think you "should" be after in life), the universe will align itself in service to what you want. So what can you do instead of searching and trying? Relax-Trust- Affirm-Receive."

"Make an effort to find the positive side in all things we do. There are so many people in the world who steal joy from others. LET'S PAY IT FORWARD AND FIND THE JOY IN ALL THINGS."

"I pray that everyone has love in their hearts and understand that joy comes from inner peace. Remember, if you want to never fail stay close to Gods word as he will keep you as he has never failed anyone. His love won't fail you. So thank you God for never failing me or those that I love."

"In life all we need is love and health. And always remember God will always give us what we NEED but we have to work for what we WANT! Live life to the fullest because you never know what tomorrow will bring."

"So many people PRAY for opportunity and when they get it they MESS it up. And then there's the people who HATE on people who have what they wish they did, and when given the opportunity, ain't ready for whatever reason. Haters exist to prove that others do what it takes to prepare."

"Thank you for a wonderful life. Without your divine presence and guidance I am lost. Your eternal love saves me, and your mercy is relentless. As trouble and stress drive me to prayer, let my prayers drive away trouble and stress. Amen"

"People will tell you that you must forgive, but forgiveness don't always mean the relationship is going to improve. There are just some people that are not capable of forgiveness or of love, so it might be wise to just let them be angry. So wish them well, and let them go on their way."

"Many have become my enemies without cause, those who hate me without reason are numerous. Those who repay my good with evil lodge accusations against me though I seek only to do what is good...Psalms 38:19-20

"To get a new outcome you must do things in a new way. So visualize yourself achieving your goals if you want to make them happen. The old me would have just rolled with it, the new me won't. I have grown and I thank you for helping me GROW."

"What we in our hearts and minds believe or long for, becomes manifest in our reality. The Law of Attraction states that we draw to ourselves vibrationally anything that we focus on.... or "like attracts like". So we manifest into our reality that what we focus upon."

"I cannot imagine where I would be today were it not for some of my friends, friends who have given me a heart full of joy. Face it people, friends make life a lot more fun." Blessed are they who have the gift of making friends, for it is one of God's greatest gifts."

"When they counted you out, you won, when they wouldn't help you, you did it without them. When you stood in the winner's circle, you thanked God. Only your true father has you covered."

"Blessed folk irritate haters."

"A wise man once said you must be graceful under pressure, as it will make you happy. The state of grace that surrounds you will then allow you to appreciate and honor everyone and everything around you."

"If someone helps you get where you can't get alone it is not them but GOD working it all out. Your heart must be in it with no expectations of a return and that is how you keep getting blessed."

"Look for the blessing in every challenge and you'll have a much better experience."

"Many folks say trust your gut. Trusting your gut can steer you wrong. Pray and being guided by the Holy Spirit will see you through every time. I have trusted my gut and it has gotten me nowhere fast."

"As the Holiday season is upon, many people tend to forget that happiness doesn't come as a result of getting something you don't have, but rather of recognizing and appreciating what you do have."

"I been still, real still and waited on the Lord, and as it is written, he has delivered."

"Smile and laugh as much as you can help someone out you may or may not know. Life is very precious and I thank God every day for what he has given to me, and so should you."

"Everything you want is out there waiting for you to ask. Everything you want also wants you. So in the end, what you are looking for is also looking for you."

"A wise man once said that the secret to success is attuning your limited, human will to the infinite divine will."

"Stay on course with your current decisions for your dreams cannot manifest if you have doubt about the result you want as a double minded man is unstable in all his ways."

"The devil will sometimes give you a present. All gifts are not worth having. If all you care about is what you gonna get, you just may get something you did not bargain for."

"Real men will sacrifice to get things in order, and getting things in order allows for the divine order of God to bless them"

"Life presents many things that we are unable to comprehend. We have to trust that God allows us to go through struggle(s) so that we may progress to a better place."

"I urge you to do what you can to create more harmony between the versions of yourself that you project outward and the version of yourself you actually live in."

"Don't ever stop speaking things into existence, even when it seems unlikely, even things that seem impossible eventually manifest into reality"

"A man is willing to stand in the presence of confederates and confront them. If you cannot say the comments in the presence of those you speak about, then retreat to your proper place."

"I am too old to ever see the tree that will grow from this seed. But I know that those who follow me will eat from its fruit."

"If someone wants to walk away from being in your life let them. A manifest destiny is never connected to the person that leaves you."

"People always telling lies thinking they messing up someone's life. If you really want to mess up somebody, tell them the truth"

"You are only hurting yourself when you judge people and speak negatively. You stop the flow of positive energy towards you."

"If you ask for help, please be ready to accept it."

"Be more inclined to count your blessings instead of complaining about what you don't have."

"God has created a lane specifically for you. Embrace your unique qualities and let your light shine."

"Either you go hard with serving God or someone else will be getting your blessings."

"A loving heart is forever young."

"The devil always wants something for nothing. In most cases he's getting it done with superstar recruiters!"

"Is it really necessary to blow out someone else's light in order to let your own light shine?"

"God is Supreme. In order to change your ways you must change your thoughts." (Isaiah 55 summarized.)

"Thanking those that bless you is required in order to keep getting blessed."

"I am where I am because of you. I am what I am because of you. I will do what I do because of you. Shine your light on me."

THE END

ABOUT THE AUTHOR

Anonymous.

* 9 7 8 0 9 9 8 3 7 3 8 1 2 *